AMERICAN CURRENT AFFAIRS:

What you need to know about the United States

By:

Beverly T. Boyd

TABLE OF CONTENT

SECTION 1: U.S. HOLIDAYS & CELEBRATIONS

The United States, like other countries, sets aside several days each year to memorialize events, personalities, or public occurrences. These holidays normally are characterized by a broad cessation of work and economic activity, and by public and/or religious rituals.

Technically, the United States does not observe national holidays, but Congress has designated 10 "legal public holidays," during which most government institutions are closed and most federal workers are excused from work. Although individual states and private enterprises are not obligated to respect them, in fact, all states, and virtually all employers, observe the bulk of them.

Since 1971, a few of these have been scheduled on Mondays rather than on a specific calendar day to provide employees with a long holiday weekend.

New Year's Day (January 1) (January 1)

Birthday of Martin Luther King Jr. (third Monday in January) (third Monday in January)

African American History Month

Washington's Birthday (third Monday in February) (third Monday in February)

National Women's History Month

Memorial Day Holiday (last Monday in May) (last Monday, May)

Independence Day (July 4) (July 4)

Labor Day (first Monday in September) (first Monday in September)

Hispanic Heritage Month (September 15 - October 15) (September 15 - October 15)

Columbus Day (second Monday in October) (second Monday in October)

National Native American Heritage Month

Veterans Day (November 11) (November 11)

Thanksgiving Day (fourth Thursday in November) (fourth Thursday in November)

World AIDS Day (December 1) (December 1)

Human Rights Day (December 10) (December 10)

Christmas Day (December 25) (December 25)

SECTION 2: IMPORTANT MOMENTS IN THE HISTORY OF THE UNITED STATES

Dividing history into decades is an arbitrary but often highly effective approach to attempting to grasp the arcs and impact of events. Trying to pinpoint any particular event as essential to the knowledge of a specific decade maybe even more arbitrary. It is subjective. Nevertheless, that endeavor may at the very least be a spark for debate. What follows is an effort to identify decade-defining milestones in the history of the United States from the country's foundation.

The 1770s: Declaration of Independence (1776) (1776)

The relevance of the Declaration of Independence (1776) to the history of the 1770s is self-evident. From the Boston Tea Party to the shot heard around the world, Washington's Crossing of Delaware, and the Valley Forge winter, the American Revolution's quest for liberty was made real by the foundational text of the great American experiment in democracy.

The 1780s: Constitution of the United States of America (1787) (1787)

With the war won, independence secured, and the Articles of Confederation proving inadequate, the Founding Fathers laid down the law by which the new country would be governed in the elegantly crafted Constitution, which, depending upon one's perspective, was meant to either evolve to meet changing circumstances or to be strictly interpreted to adhere to the Founders' "original intent."

The 1790s: Whiskey Rebellion (1794) (1794)

As the new country began finding its feet, U.S. Pres. George Washington sent troops to western Pennsylvania in 1794 to quell the Whiskey Rebellion, an uprising by citizens who refused to pay a liquor tax that had been imposed by Secretary of Treasury Alexander Hamilton to raise money for the national debt and to assert the power of the national government. Federalists welcomed the victory of national power; members of the Thomas Jefferson's Republican (later Democratic-Republican) Party were dismayed by what they perceived as government overreach. More than two centuries later, the names and faces have changed, but the tale is continuous.

The 1800s: Louisiana Purchase (1803) (1803)

The Louisiana Territory, the huge swath of land (more than 800,000 square miles) that made up the western Mississippi basin, passed from French colonial rule to Spanish colonial rule and then back to the French before U.S. Pres. Thomas Jefferson pried it away from Napoleon in 1803 for a final price of some $27 million. Out of it were carved—in their entirety—the states of Louisiana, Missouri, Arkansas, Iowa, North

Dakota, South Dakota, Nebraska, and Oklahoma along with much of Kansas, Colorado, Wyoming, Montana, and Minnesota. Exploring the territory obtained by the Louisiana Purchase also gave Lewis and Clark something to do for two years.

The 1810s: Battle of New Orleans (1815) (1815)

On January 8, 1815, a motley army under the direction of Andrew Jackson successfully beats British troops in the Battle of New Orleans, even though the War of 1812 had already concluded. News of the Treaty of Ghent (December 24, 1814) had yet to reach the combatants. The American triumph produced a national hero of future president Jackson and contributed to the public notion that the U.S. had won the war, although in actuality the struggle was virtually a draw, and the problems that had brought it on remained largely unsolved.

The 1820s: Monroe Doctrine (1823) (1823)

The Era of Good Feelings (approximately 1815–25), an era of American prosperity and isolationism, was in full swing when U.S. Pres. James Monroe outlined a set of beliefs in 1823 that decades later would be named the Monroe Doctrine. According to the policy, the United States would not meddle in European politics, but equally, it would not permit additional European colonialism in the Americas or European meddling in the governments of the American continent. It is dubious if the U.S. at the time had the strength to back up its swagger, but later, as a global power, it would apply a wide application of the concept in its "sphere of influence."

The 1830s: Era of the Common Man (1829–37) (1829–37)

Andrew Jackson, the U.S. president from 1829–37, was considered to have ushered in the Era of the Common Man. But although suffrage had been substantially extended beyond men of property, it was not a consequence of Jackson's efforts. Despite the intentional spread of his image as a champion of popular democracy and as a man of the people, he was far more inclined to connect himself with the influential not with the have-nots, with the creditor not with the debtor. Jacksonian democracy spoke a fine game for people on the street but offered nothing.

1840s: Treaty of Guadalupe Hidalgo (1848) (1848)

Signed on February 2, 1848, the Treaty of Guadalupe Hidalgo brought to a close the Mexican-American War (1846–48) and seemingly fulfilled the Manifest Destiny of the United States championed by Pres. James K. Polk by adding 525,000 square miles (1,360,000 square km) of formerly Mexican land to the U.S. territory.

The 1850s: Dred Scott Decision (1857) (1857)

The 1850s were saturated with harbingers of the American Civil War to come—from the Compromise of 1850, which briefly forestalled North-South hostilities, to John Brown's Harpers Ferry Raid, which drove them up. Arguably, however, by fanning abolitionist outrage in an increasingly split society, the U.S. Supreme Court's Dred Scott decision set the deck for the 1860 election of Abraham Lincoln as president, which eventually caused secession and war.

The 1860s: Battle of Gettysburg (1863) (1863)

In July 1863, the year of the Emancipation Proclamation, in the little Pennsylvania crossroads town of Gettysburg, Robert E. Lee's invading Army of Northern Virginia endured a loss so severe that it sealed the fate of the Confederacy and its "peculiar institution." Within two years the war was done, and by the end of the decade, the South was briefly altered by Reconstruction.

The 1870s: Battle of the Little Bighorn (1876) (1876)

While the nation celebrated its centennial at the Philadelphia Centennial Exposition, on June 25, 1876, the 7th Cavalry under the command of Col. George Armstrong Custer was defeated by Lakota and Northern

Cheyenne warriors commanded by Sitting Bull in the Battle of the Little Bighorn. Although it was a great success for the Northern Plains people against U.S. expansionism, the war signaled the beginning of the collapse of Native American sovereignty over the West.

1880s: Haymarket Riot (1886) (1886)

The wealth-concentrating methods of the "robber barons" who managed the boom of industrial activity and corporate expansion during the Gilded Age of the late 19th century were challenged by the advent of organized labor headed by the Knights of Labor. However, when a protest gathering relating to one of the roughly 1,600 strikes held throughout 1886 was disturbed by the explosion of a bomb that killed seven policemen at the Haymarket Riot, many people blamed the violence on organized labor, which fell into decline until the turn of the century.

The 1890s: Plessy v. Ferguson (1896) (1896)

With the conclusion of Reconstruction in the 1870s, the adoption of Jim Crow laws reinforced racial segregation in the South. In its 7–1 decision in the Plessy v. Ferguson case in May 1896, the U.S. Supreme Court gave constitutional sanction to laws designed to achieve racial segregation utilizing separate and supposedly equal public facilities and services for African Americans and whites, thus providing a controlling judicial precedent that would endure until the 1950s.

The 1900s: Breakup of Northern Securities (1902–04) (1902–04) (1902–04)
In 1902 U.S. Pres. Theodore Roosevelt pursued the Progressive goal of curbing the enormous economic and political power of the giant corporate trusts by resurrecting the nearly defunct Sherman Antitrust Act to bring a lawsuit that led to the breakup of a huge railroad conglomerate, the Northern Securities Company (ordered by the U.S. Supreme Court in 1904). (ordered by the U.S. Supreme Court in 1904). (ordered by

the U.S. Supreme Court in 1904). Roosevelt maintained this campaign of "trust-busting" by bringing actions against 43 more prominent firms throughout the following seven years.

The 1910s: Sinking of the Lusitania (1915) (1915) (1915)
As World War I raged in Europe, most Americans, including U.S. Pres. Woodrow Wilson, were committed to avoiding involvement and dedicated to neutrality, although the U.S. economy had gained greatly by shipping food, raw material, weaponry, and ammunition to the Allies. More than any other single episode, the sinking of the unarmed British ocean liner, the Lusitania, by a German submarine on May 7, 1915 (killing, among others, 128 Americans), led the U.S. to join the war on the side of the Allies. Leaving aside its isolationism, the U.S. became a global force, but by the decade's end, it would shrink from involvement in the growing League of Nations.

The 1920s: Stock Market Crash (1929) (1929) (1929)

"The major business of the American people is business," U.S. Pres. Calvin Coolidge remarked in 1925. And with the American economy humming during the "Roaring Twenties" (the Jazz Age), peace and prosperity prevailed in the United States...until they didn't. The era came to a close in October 1929 when the stock market crashed, setting the stage for years of economic suffering and tragedy during the Great Depression.

The 1930s: FDR's First Fireside Chat (1933) (1933) (1933)

In 1933 at least one-fourth of the U.S. workforce was unemployed when the administration of Pres. Franklin D. Roosevelt first took on the ravages of the Great Depression with the New Deal, a federal government program that sought to bring about immediate economic relief as well as reforms in industry, agriculture, finance, labor, and housing. On March 12, 1933, Roosevelt gave the first in a long series (1933–44) of straightforward informal radio addresses, the fireside chats, which were initially intended to garner support for the New Deal but eventually contributed to reformulating the American social mentality from one of despair to one of hope during a time of multiple crises, including the Great Depression and World War II.

The 1940s: The Atomic Bombing of Hiroshima and Nagasaki (1945) (1945) (1945)

Having again remained out of the opening stages of another international battle, the U.S. entered World War II on the side of the Allies following the Japanese attack on Pearl Harbor (December 1941). (December 1941). (December 1941). In August 1945, with the war in Europe over and U.S. forces advancing on Japan, U.S. Pres. Harry S. Truman ushered in the nuclear era by choosing to drop atomic bombs on Hiroshima and Nagasaki, Japan, in the hope that the terrible destruction unleashed would prevent an even greater loss of life than seemed likely with a protracted island-by-island invasion of Japan.

The 1950s: U.S. Army–McCarthy Hearings (1954) (1954) (1954)

With the Cold War as a backdrop, U.S. Sen. Joseph McCarthy gave his name to an era (McCarthyism) by fanning the flames of anti-communist hysteria with sensational but unproven charges of communist subversion in high government circles. At the same time, the House Un-American Activities Committee investigated alleged communist activities in the entertainment industry. McCarthy's power diminished in 1954 when a nationally aired 36-day hearing on his charges of subversion by U.S. Army personnel and civilian authorities showed his harsh interrogative procedures.

The 1960s: Assassination of Martin Luther King, Jr. (1968) (1968) (1968)

At the center of the huge social and political turbulence of the 1960s were the civil rights movement, opposition to the Vietnam War, the creation of youth-oriented counterculture, and the establishment and conservative parties that pushed back against change. The April 4, 1968, slaying of Martin Luther King, Jr., the most known civil rights leader, demonstrated the terrible, lethal implications that may develop from a country's political split.

The 1970s: Watergate Scandal (1972–74) (1972–74) (1972–74)
On August 9, 1974—facing probable impeachment for his involvement in covering up the scandal surrounding the break-in at the Democratic National Committee (DNC) headquarters at the Watergate complex in Washington, D.C., in June 1972—Republican Richard Nixon became the only U.S. president to resign. The loss of faith in government officials from the scandal soaked both popular and political culture with dread and disillusion over the decade.

The 1980s: PATCO Strike (1981) (1981) (1981)

U.S. Pres. Ronald Reagan's win over the strike by the Professional Air Traffic Controllers Organization (PATCO) in August 1981 played a crucial role in the long-term erosion of the influence of labor unions and helped create the pace for his administration. Reagan's ascension to the presidency in 1980 had much to do with his linguistic abilities to clear the cloud of gloom caused by Watergate. This supported his efforts to establish supply-side (monetarist) economic policies founded on the belief that decreasing taxes on wealthy "job creators" would generate a rising tide that would lift all boats. Critics complained that the wealth obtained throughout the decade never "trickled down" to the rank and file.

The 1990s: The Monica Lewinsky Affair (1998–99) (1998–99) (1998–99)

Having failed to push through several high-profile policy initiatives early in his first term as president and confronted with Republican majorities in both houses of Congress after the 1994 midterm election, Democrat Bill Clinton pivoted toward political accommodation, oversaw a robust economy, and reversed the spiraling budget deficit. Nonetheless, his affair with a White House intern, Monica Lewinsky, led to his impeachment in December 1998, though he was convicted on charges of perjury and obstruction of justice

The 2000s: September 11 Attacks

Although terrorist attacks had been directed at the United States at the end of the 20th century, a new sense of vulnerability was introduced into American life on September 11, 2001, when Islamist terrorists crashed hijacked planes into the World Trade Center in New York City, the Pentagon in Washington, D.C., and the Pennsylvania countryside, resulting in the deaths of nearly 3,000 people.

The 2010s: Election of Donald Trump (2016) (2016) (2016)

Since at least the 1980s, the U.S. had been politically polarized by so-called culture wars that symbolically divided the country into Republican-dominated red states (typically characterized as conservative, God-fearing, pro-life, and opposed to big government and same-sex marriage) and Democrat-dominated blue states (theoretically liberal, secular, politically correct, and pro-choice) (theoretically liberal, secular, politically correct, and pro-choice) (theoretically liberal, secular, politically correct, and pro-choice). The 2016 election of Republican Donald Trump—whose campaign was grounded in nationalism and anti-immigrant rhetoric—could be seen then as a reaction to the seeming triumph of "blue" values during the two-term presidency (2009–17) of the United States' first African American president, Democrat Barack Obama.

SECTION 3: HISTORICAL EVENTS IN THE HEALTH AND HUMAN SERVICES OF THE USA

The U.S. Department of Health and Human Services (HHS) is the nation's premier department for preserving the health of all Americans and delivering important human services.

Below is a list of important events in HHS history and a list of the Secretaries of HHS/HEW.

2010
The Affordable Care Act was signed into law, making extensive U.S. health insurance changes.

2003

The Medicare Prescription Drug Improvement and Modernization Act of 2003 was passed - the most substantial expansion of Medicare since its creation. It offered a prescription medicine benefit.

2002
The Office of Public Health Emergency Preparedness (formerly the Office of the Assistant Secretary for Preparedness and Response) was founded to coordinate efforts against bioterrorism and other emergency health threats.

2001
The Centers for Medicare & Medicaid was founded, replacing the Health Care Financing Administration.HHS reacts to the nation's first bioterrorism incident - transmission of anthrax via the mail.

2000
Publication of human genome sequencing.

1999
The Ticket to Work and Work Incentives Improvement Act of 1999 was signed, making it possible for millions of Americans

with disabilities to join the workforce without fear of losing their Medicaid and Medicare coverage. It also modernized the employment services system for people with disabilities.

An initiative to combat bioterrorism was launched.

1997

The State Children's Health Insurance Program (SCHIP) was created, enabling states to extend health coverage to more uninsured children.

1996

Welfare reform under the Personal Responsibility and Work Opportunity Reconciliation Act was enacted.

The Health Insurance Portability and Accountability Act (HIPAA) was enacted.

1995
The Social Security Administration became an independent agency.

1993
Vaccines for Children Program was established, providing free immunizations to all children in low-income families.

1990
Human Genome Project was established.

Nutrition Labeling and Education Act was passed, authorizing the food label.

Ryan White Comprehensive AIDS Resource Emergency (CARE) Act began providing support for people with HIV/AIDS

1989

The Agency for Health Care Policy and Research (now the Agency for Healthcare Research and Quality) was created.

1988

JOBS program and federal support for child care was created.

McKinney Act was passed to provide health care to the homeless.

1984

National Organ Transplantation Act was signed into law.
1981

Identification of AIDS - In 1984, HIV was identified by the Public Health Service and French scientists. In 1985, a blood test to detect HIV was licensed.

1980

Federal funding was provided to states for foster care and adoption assistance.

1979

The Department of Education Organization Act was signed into law, providing for a separate Department of Education. The Department of Health, Education, and Welfare (HEW) became the Department of Health and Human Services (HHS) on May 4, 1980.

1977

The Health Care Financing Administration was created to manage Medicare and Medicaid separately from the Social Security Administration.

Worldwide eradication of smallpox, led by the U.S. Public Health Service.

1975

Child Support Enforcement and Paternity Establishment Program was established.

1971

National Cancer Act was passed into law.

1970

National Health Service Corps was founded.

1966

The International Smallpox Eradication program was launched.

Community Health Center and Migrant Health Center initiatives were created.

1965

Medicare and Medicaid programs were founded, making comprehensive health care accessible to millions of Americans.

Older Americans Act developed the nutritional and social services run by HHS' Administration on Aging.

Head Start program was founded.

1964

Release of the first Surgeon General's Report on Smoking and Health.

1962

The migrant Health Act was approved, assisting with clinics serving agricultural laborers.

1961

First White House Conference on Aging.

1955

Licensing of the Salk polio vaccine.

Indian Health Service was transferred to HHS from the Department of the Interior.

1953

The Cabinet-level Department of Health, Education, and Welfare (HEW) was formed under President Eisenhower, formally coming into existence on April 11, 1953. In 1979, the Department of Education Organization Act was enacted into law, allowing for a distinct Department of Education. HEW became the Department of

Health and Human Services, formally debuting on May 4, 1980.

1946
Communicable Disease Center was created, a precursor of the Centers for Disease Control and Prevention.

1939
The Government Security Agency was founded, bringing together linked federal initiatives in the domains of health, education, and social insurance.

1938
Federal Food, Drug, and Cosmetic Act were approved.

1935
Social Security Act was approved.

1930

The National Institute (later Institutes) of Health was founded out of the Public Health Service's Hygienic Laboratory.

1921

The Bureau of Indian Affairs Health Division, the precursor of the Indian Health Service, was founded.

1912

President Theodore Roosevelt's first White House Conference suggested the formation of the Children's Bureau to address the exploitation of children.

1906

The Pure Food and Drugs Act was approved, empowering the government to oversee the purity of foods and the safety of medications, currently a duty of the FDA.

1902

Conversion of the Marine Hospital Service into the Public Health and Marine Hospital Service in acknowledgment of its expanded efforts in the sphere of public health. In 1912, the name was reduced to the Public Health Service.

1891

Immigration law was approved, allocating the Marine Hospital Service the obligation for medical assessment of incoming immigrants.

1887

The federal government constructed a one-room laboratory on Staten Island for the study of illness, a very early forerunner of the National Institutes of Health.

1878

The National Quarantine Act was approved, commencing the transfer of quarantine activities from the states to the federal Marine Hospital Service.

1871

Appointment of the first Supervising Surgeon (later named the Surgeon General) for the Marine Hospital Service, which had been formed the preceding year.

1862

President Lincoln nominated a scientist, Charles M. Wetherill, to serve in the new Department of Agriculture. This was the commencement of the Bureau of Chemistry, the predecessor of the Food and Drug Administration.

1798

Passage of an act for the relief of ill and injured sailors, which created a government network of hospitals for the treatment of merchant seamen, the predecessor of today's U.S. Public Health Service.

Secretaries of HHS and HEW

The Secretary is a member of the President's Cabinet. Nominations to the post of Secretary are forwarded to the U.S. Senate Committee on Health, Education, Labor, and Pensions, as well as the U.S. Senate Committee on Finance. Confirmation is last examined by the U.S. Senate.

January 24, 2018 - January 20, 2021

Alex M. Azar II exit disclaimer icon

February 10, 2017 - September 29, 2017

Thomas E. Price, M.D. (Archive Collection exit disclaimer icon) (Archive Collection exit disclaimer icon)
June 9, 2014 - January 20, 2017

Sylvia M. Burwell exit disclaimer icon (Archive Collection exit disclaimer icon) (Archive Collection exit disclaimer icon)

April 28, 2009 - June 6, 2014

Kathleen Sebelius exit disclaimer icon (Archive Collection exit disclaimer icon) (Archive Collection exit disclaimer icon)

January 26, 2005 - January 20, 2009

Michael O. Leavitt exit disclaimer icon (Archive Collection exit disclaimer symbol) (Archive Collection exit disclaimer icon)

February 2, 2001 - January 26, 2005

Tommy G. Thompson departure disclaimer icon

January 22, 1993 - January 20, 2001

Donna E. Shalala exit disclaimer icon

March 1, 1989 - January 20, 1993
 Louis W. Sullivan, M.D
December 13, 1985 - January 20, 1989

 Otis R. Bowen, M.D.

March 9, 1983 - December 13, 1985

 Margaret M. Heckler

January 22, 1981 - February 3, 1983

 Richard S. Schweiker

August 3, 1979 - January 20, 1981

 Patricia Roberts Harris

January 25, 1977 - August 3, 1979

 Joseph A. Califano, Jr.

August 8, 1975 - January 20, 1977

David Mathews
February 12, 1973 - August 8, 1975
Caspar W. Weinberger

June 24, 1970 - January 29, 1973

Elliot L. Richardson

January 21, 1969 - June 23, 1970

Robert H. Finch

May 16, 1968 - January 20, 1969

Wilbur J. Cohen

August 18, 1965 - March 1, 1968

John W. Gardner

July 31, 1962 - August 17, 1965

Anthony J. Celebrezze

January 21, 1961 - July 13, 1962

Abraham Ribicoff

August 1, 1958 - January 19, 1961

Arthur S. Flemming

August 1, 1955 - July 31, 1958

Marion B. Folsom

April 11, 1953 - July 31, 1955

SECTION 4: CURRENT AFFAIRS IN THE UNITED STATES

U.S. Temporarily Suspends 'Green Cards & Non-Migrant Work Visas' till 31st December 2020

Following a global economic crisis since COVID-19 was declared a pandemic back in March 2020, the United States Government has decided to suspend 'Green Cards and Non-Migrant Work Visas' till the 31st of December 2020 to protect jobs for the citizens of the United States.

The executive order was signed by United States President Donald Trump on 22nd June 2020.

Contents

Background
Suspended Work Visas

Reform in H-1B Visa Programme Impact on India

Background
The suspension of Green Card and Non-migrant work visas will create around 5,25,000 jobs in the United States. Due to COVID-19, as per reports, a record 47 million could lose their jobs in the United States.

Suspended Work Visas
H-1B
H-4 for some H-1B spouses
H-2B for low-skill workers
L-1 for Intra-Company Transfers
J Visas for Educational and Cultural Workers
Reform in H-1B Visa Programme
President Donald Trump also instructed his administration to make reforms in the current H-1B Visa Programme. As per the reform, immigrant workers who are offered the highest wages by the recruiter shall be given priority, this is to ensure that the wages of United States citizens are protected as employers will not be able to recruit low-cost foreign labor.

Until today, the H-1B visas were distributed through a random lottery.

Impact on India
Every year H-1B Visas are issued to 85,000 only, out of these, as per the records the largest beneficiaries of the visa program were the Indians. More than 70 percent of the total 85,000 beneficiaries are from India.

U.S. Russia talks on new Nuclear Disarmament Treaty begin without China

Delegations from the United States led by Marshall Billingslea and the Russian Delegation under their Foreign Minister Sergei Ryabkov begin their 2-day talks on 22nd June 2020 at the capital city of Austria, Vienna. The talks for extending the nuclear disarmament treaty were in doubt over the last few months as United States President Donald Trump continued the call for the addition of China to the treaty. The treaty is commonly known by the name 'START' treaty.

Contents

China's Response to Trump Call

According to China, It's still not the right time for them to be involved or to be a part of such a nuclear treaty, the United States and Russia have the primary responsibility of nuclear disarmament as the nuclear stockpile of China is dwarfed by those of the two countries.

China also added that for other nations to join the Nuclear Disarmament Treaty, the United States must drastically reduce the size of its stockpile.

START Treaty

START (Strategic Arms Reduction Treaty) is a bilateral nuclear disarmament treaty between the United States and Russia. The formal name of the treaty is 'Measures for the Further Reduction and Limitation of Strategic Offensive Arms.

The treaty was last signed on 8th April 2010 and came into effect on 5th February 2011 for 10 years. The current treaty expires on 5th February 2021.

Russia's Energia plans to take the First Tourist on Space Walk in 2023

On 25th June 2020, Russian Company- S.P. Korolev Rocket and Space Corporation Energia (also known as RSC Energia) announced that it will take the first tourist for a spacewalk in 2023. The announcement came after RSC Energia signed a deal with Space Adventures (a space tourism company in the United States). RSC Energia is a part of the Roscosmos (Russia's space agency).

As per the deal, two tourists will be sent to the International Space Station (ISS) in the year 2023 under the joint agreement of both companies. From the end of RSC Energia, one of the two tourists will be able to do a spacewalk together with a cosmonaut from Roscosmos.

Between 2001 to 2009, Space Adventures along with the Russian Space Agency has taken eight tourists to the ISS. In 2001,

Dennis Tito (a businessman from the United States) became the World's First Private Space Explorer (the first paying space tourist in the world). Since 2009, no other space tourist program has been conducted in the world. None of the space tourists to date have done a spacewalk.

Background

The announcement came a month after SpaceX (the United States-based space transportation services and aerospace manufacturer company) broke the monopoly of the Russian space agency. Until 30th May 2020, only the Russian Space Agency Roscosmos had the technology to successfully able to carry Humans to space. All Human Space Flight missions until 30th May 2020 were conducted with the help of the Russian crew spacecraft Soyuz. On 30th May 2020, the Falcon 9 rocket of SpaceX successfully carried two astronauts from NASA to the ISS.

SpaceX in February 2020 also signed an agreement with Space Adventures. Under the agreement, both companies have planned to carry out a space tourism trip next year. The number of space tourists for the trip will be 3. Spacewalk for the tourists on this trip is not a part of the agreement yet.

Daniel Lewis Lee: First Federal Execution in the US in 17 years

The United States Justice Department has said that Daniel Lewis Lee (47), convicted of killing three persons of a family, was put to death by lethal injection. This is the first federal execution in the nation in the previous 17 years.

Daniel is the first of the three federal offenders who are likely to be executed this week for multiple offenses.

Capital Punishment in the USA

Capital punishment is commonly administered in the USA and it is the only sophisticated western country that still retains this provision in its legislation. In reality, the USA was the first nation to devise a fatal injection for execution reasons and since then, five other countries have also embraced this. The practice is presently followed in 28 US states, the federal government, and even the US Military.

However, there has been tremendous outrage in the worldwide community for the abolition of the death penalty / capital punishment with the United Nations approving a resolution to that effect in 2007. However, several nations have yet to accept and execute it.

US bans Foreign Students taking Online Courses from Entry to the Country

The US President has issued new criteria that are going to ban any new student wanting to accept admission in the online-only study from entering the United States. Immigration and Customs Enforcement has confirmed that non-immigrant students in new or initial status after March 9 would not be eligible to enter the nation in a US school as a non-immigrant student for the autumn term to pursue a full course of study that is online.

The designated schools will also not distribute the needed paperwork to the non-immigrant students in the new or initial status who are outside the US and intend to attend courses at a Student and Exchange Visitor Program-certified educational institution completely online.

These rules have been published after the previous criteria practically sent thousands of students home from graduate institutions to even primary schools in the nation. 17 states and the District of Columbia filed a lawsuit against the regulation fearing a decline in the foreign students in most of the renowned colleges in the country.

CARAT: Joint Naval Exercise between Bangladesh and US

On November 4, 2020, Bangladesh and the United States staged a combined Naval Exercise CARAT. CARAT is Cooperation Afloat Readiness and Training. The exercise was conducted in Chittagong.

Contents

Highlights

About the Exercise

Role of UNODC in the exercise

CARAT
Significance of Chittagong to India

Highlights

Historically, the exercise incorporates people-to-people encounters, diversity of professional exchanges, community relations projects, Subject Matter Expert exchanges, and social activities. Due to COVID-19, the exercise was held virtually.

About the Exercise

Certain events of the exercise are to be held virtually. It comprises Maritime Domain Awareness, Replenishment at Sea training, legal rules at sea, and aviation best practices of Unmanned Aerial Vehicles. This is the first year, the exercise is sponsored by the United Nations Office of Drugs and Crime and the Bali Process Regional Support Office.

Role of UNODC in the exercise

The UNODC will instruct technical support to fight maritime crime and the smuggling of migrants.
CARAT

It is a series of yearly bilateral military exercises undertaken by the US Pacific fleet with nations such as Bangladesh, Cambodia, Brunei, Indonesia, Philippines, Malaysia, Sri Lanka, Singapore, and Thailand. The emphasis of the exercise is mostly on ASEAN. However, it is also conducted with non-ASEAN countries such as Sri Lanka and Bangladesh.

This year, Bangladesh was the second to conduct the exercise after Brunei. CARAT Brunei was held in the South China sea between October 5 and October 9, 2020.

Significance of Chittagong to India

The port is critically essential for North East India.

In 2015, India and Bangladesh announced arrangements to utilize the Chittagong port for the transshipment of products from and to India. In October 2018, the governments inked arrangements to utilize Mongla port for the transshipment of products.

Eight routes were granted under the agreement to facilitate access to the North East Region through Bangladesh.

This would assist minimize time, distance, and logistical costs for the transit of commodities from India to the North Eastern area.

Stopgap Funding Bill

US President Donald Trump has signed the Stopgap Funding Bill. The measure offers the lawmakers two additional days to settle certain difficulties in the current discussions regarding the 900 billion USD assistance package.

Contents

What is the Stopgap Funding Bill?

How does the Federal Funding expire?
What is termed Government Shutdown?

Impacts on the Public

What is the Stopgap Funding Bill?

A stopgap funding bill is used by the US Government to guarantee that it does not run out of cash for conducting government programs beyond the deadline of an Appropriation Act. In a fiscal year, the US Congress adopts 12 Appropriation Acts which grant budgetary authorization to spend from the US Treasury for certain reasons. These Acts have a deadline and the money cannot be utilized to satisfy additional responsibilities after it. When Congress fails to finance the government, a government shutdown is proclaimed and all non-essential functions are suspended.

How does the Federal Funding expire?
The Fiscal year in the US starts on October 1. During a fiscal year, Congress approves twelve yearly appropriation acts that give the budget power to use monies from US Treasury for certain purposes. The cash cannot be utilized to cover additional liabilities. In other words, the monies expire after a set period.

What is termed Government Shutdown?

The Government Shutdown happens when Congress fails to finance the government. In such an event, the US Government shuts down all non-essential services. On the other hand, the necessary services such as police agencies, military forces, etc remain in operation.

The longest Government Shutdown in US history occurred during the Trump administration when the Government was shut down for thirty-five days between December 2018 and February 2019. The closure happened over a disagreement over the border wall financing.

Impacts on the Public
The Government Shutdowns in the United States have resulted in furloughs for several hundred thousand Government Employees. The decline in Government activity affects several areas of the economy.

National Defence Authorisation Act, 2021

The National Defence Authorisation act, of 2021 was adopted by the United States to establish the budget, spending, and policies of the United States Department of Defence for the fiscal year 2021. The statute established the yearly budget of the United States as 740.5 USD. The first National Defence authorization act, 2021 was approved in 1961. Since then, the measure has been approved every year.

Contents

Why is the act named after William M Thornberry?

What is the latest problem with the National Defence authorization act?

What are the Veto powers of the US President?

Why is the act named after William M Thornberry?

The measure has been dubbed the William M Thornberry National Defence authorization act. It has been named after William m Thornberry to commemorate him. He served as the chair of the house armed services committee. The committee is responsible for financing and supervising the department of Defence in the United States.

What is the latest problem with the National Defence authorization act?

The departing US President Donald Trump has rejected the National Defence Authorisation act, 2021 stating that the measure endangered national security. He also disapproved of its requirements of designating military locations after confederate commanders. However, the House of Representatives decided to override the veto authority of President Trump.

What are the Veto powers of the US President?

The President of the United States may opt to veto or reject the law on rare instances. However, the parliamentarians may overcome the Veto and adopt measures into law by demonstrating two-thirds of votes in both Chambers of Congress.

Every Bill for the resolution adopted by the United States Congress is forwarded to the president for his approval. Once the measure is delivered, the president may sign the bill into law within 10 days or may reject the bill by returning to Congress with grounds of concern. If the president does not do anything with the bill, the measure automatically becomes law after 10 days.

 The word Veto does not occur in the Constitution of the United States.

What is the 25th Amendment of the US Constitution?

The United States Capitol Protests, 2021, have spurred demands to invoke the 25th Constitutional amendment.

Contents

When was the 25th US Constitutional Amendment introduced?

Has the fourth provision of the 25th US Constitutional Amendment been used thus far?

Why did Trump supporters storm the US Capitol?

What is the 25th Amendment of the US Constitution?

The 25th Constitutional amendment spells forth how a US President or a Vice President may be removed or succeeded. It involves addressing concerns centering around tragic scenarios like death, resignation to the removal of the US President and procedures to be taken if a President becomes incapacitated to such a degree that he is unable to complete his obligations. The amendment comprises four parts.

What are the four parts of the amendment?

The vice president would take the post and title of the president in the case of the resignation of the president. Which will essentially preclude the leaving current from returning to the office.

The second portion of the amendment covers provisions concerning vacancies in the position of vice president.
the third part of the amendment gives provisions to decide that a city of presidents fulfills his powers and responsibilities.

 The vice president may take over as acting president if the president proclaims his or her incapacity to serve as president. When the president is unable to declare his or her incapable then the fourth provision of the amendment is applied. This provision demands the vice president and the cabinet to jointly show the incapacity of the Vice-President.

Currently, individuals and leaders of the United States of America are pressing vice president Pence to activate this fourth portion of the 25th Constitutional Amendment against President Trump.

When was the 25th US Constitutional Amendment introduced?

The 25th US Constitutional amendment was introduced in 1965 and was adopted by the states in 1967.

Has the fourth provision of the 25th US Constitutional Amendment been used thus far?

No.

Why did Trump supporters storm the US Capitol?

The Trump followers stormed the US Capitol building as Trump constantly alleged that the US Presidential Election, 2020, which he lost was rigged.

US National Rifle Association

The United States National Rifle Association has filed for bankruptcy under Chapter 11 of the bankruptcy law. The association filed for bankruptcy to avoid being probed by New York Attorney General.

Contents
Background

United States Rifle Association

American Civil War

Arms Trade Treaty

Background

The New York Attorney General has sued the National Rifle Organization in August 2020 based on charges that the association's senior leaders siphoned millions of cash for their vacations.

United States Rifle Association

It is a non-profit organization created by the civil war veterans General George Wingate and Colonel William C Church in 1871. The organization was founded to promote and encourage rifle shooting on a scientific basis. It is known as the most prominent pro-gun group in the US. The opponents think that the group is a facilitator of gun violence in the nation.

NRA teaches firearm safety and proficiency. It produces various periodicals and organizes competitive marksmanship competitions. As of December 2018, the NRA comprised more than five million members.

The primary initiatives of the NRA were the Firearm Owners Protection Act which lowered the limits of the Gun Control Act of 1968 and the Dickey amendment prevented the Centres for Disease Control and Prevention from using government funding to push for gun control.

The US National Rifle Association was created by the British National Rifle Association that was formed a year and a half earlier.

American Civil War

The American Civil War was fought between 1861 and 1865. The civil war occurred as a consequence of the long-standing slavery of Black people. The NRA is thought to be a consequence of the civil war.

Arms Trade Treaty

The National Rifle Association recently criticized the Arms Trade Treaty. The Arms Commerce Treaty is a multinational treaty that controls international trade. More than 109 states have signed the pact. The pact is an effort to restrict international commerce of conventional weapons.

United States will re-join UNHRC

The Joe Biden administration in the United States is all ready to rejoin the UN Human Rights Council. The United States withdrew from the council in the year 2018 under Presidency of the Donald Trump

Contents

Background

About UN Human Rights Council (UNHCR) (UNHCR)

UNHRC Sessions

Background

Donald Trump withdrew from the international body's major human rights because of its excessive emphasis on Israel.

Israel has received the biggest number of critical council resolutions thus far concerning any other nation.

So, the Trump administration raised the problem with the body's membership.

The members include Cuba, China, Russia, Eritrea, and Venezuela. All these nations have been accused of human rights violations.

About UN Human Rights Council (UNHCR) (UNHCR)
UNHRC is an inter-governmental organization within the UN system.

The agency is concerned with enhancing the promotion and protection of human rights around the globe.

It watches after the circumstances of human rights breaches and recommendations on the issues.

The council was founded in the year 2006 by the UN General Assembly Resolution 60/251.

The inaugural session of the council took held in 2006 three months after its formation.

The agency is active in debating all the topical human rights concerns.

The UNHRC was founded after replacing the United Nations Commission on Human Rights (UNCHR) (UNCHR).

The council includes the 47 UN Member States. The member nations are chosen by the UNGA by a direct and secret vote.

UNHRC Sessions

The UNHRC convened three regular sessions in a year. The session lasts for a total of 10 weeks. The session takes place for four weeks in March, three weeks in June, and three weeks in September. The meetings are conducted at the UN Office Geneva in Switzerland.

The US formally re-joined the Paris Climate Deal

The United States formally re-joined the Paris climate deal on February 19, 2020. It joined the deal again after 107 days it departed.

Contents

Highlights

With the return of the US, the global leaders expected that now the nation would show its seriousness since it was primarily absent for four years.

The nations are also waiting for the statement from Washington on the US's target to curb emissions of heat-trapping gases by 2030.

The president of the US, Joe Biden, has issued the executive order to reverse the withdrawal ordered by the previous President, Donald Trump.

Background

In the year 2019, the Donald Trump administration declared its departure from the Paris deal. This decree came into force on November 4, 2020. the day after the election, owing to terms in the agreement.

Paris Climate Agreement

It is an accord under the United Nations Framework Convention on Climate Change (UNFCCC) (UNFCCC). This agreement was reached in 2016 and deals with climate change mitigation, adaptation, and funding. This agreement was reached by the representatives of 196 nations. It was signed during the 21st Conference of the Parties of the UNFCCC in France. The agreement was eventually accepted by consensus in December 2015. Currently, 190 members of the UNFCCC are party to the agreement. Countries like Turkey, Iran, and Iraq are not a party to it.

Goals under Paris Agreement

Under the Paris Agreement, there is a long-term aim of maintaining the average temperature to well below 2 °C above the pre-industrial levels. It also intends to exert measures to restrict the rise to 1.5 °C. This will aid in decreasing the risks and repercussions of climate change. The agreement also intends to strengthen the capacity of parties to adjust to the detrimental repercussions of climate change. It also tries to make the flow of financing towards low greenhouse gas emissions and climate-resilient development.

US co-sponsors EU-led Resolution concerning Myanmar Human Rights

United States has co-sponsored a resolution initiated by European Union (EU) underlining persistent human rights issues in Myanmar, especially for Rohingya. It has also highlighted developments made since February 1 in the 46th session of the UN

Human Rights Council (UNHRC)
(UNHRC).

Contents

Background

Council of the European Union on March 22, 2021, imposed sanctions on 11 persons who were guilty of the military coup in Myanmar and following military & police violence against peaceful protestors. The UNHRC also urges the military to restore the democratically elected government in the nation and free those who were unjustly arrested. UNHCR also asked troops to desist from violence toward the people of Burma. UNHCR Resolution also reaffirmed the mandate of the Special Rapporteur and maintained its assistance towards Independent Investigative Mechanism in Myanmar.

United States Stand on Military Coup

US Secretary of State, Antony Blinken, imposed fresh sanctions against Bureau of Special Operations head, Lt Gen Aung Soe; chief of police of Myanmar Than Hlaing; and two army units accused of human rights violations throughout ethnic regions. The US together with the United Kingdom, Norway, and Albania endorsed wording that denounced military conduct and enhanced monitoring & reporting.

Military Coup in Myanmar

Myanmar's military proclaimed a 'state of emergency for a year by ousting the democratically elected government in Myanmar on February 1, 2021, before the newly-elected parliament was due to meet. The military also house arrested the State Counsellor of Myanmar Aung San Suu Kyi, President Win Myint, and other prominent officials who were suspected of election fraud.

United Nations Human Rights Council (UNHRC)

UNHCR is a United Nations organization that promotes and preserves human rights around the globe. It consisted of 47 members chosen for a three-year term on a regional group basis. It is based in Geneva, Switzerland. The agency examines claims of abuses of human rights among the United Nations member nations. It also looks after topical human rights problems such as freedom of association and assembly, freedom of belief & religion, freedom of speech, LGBT rights, women's rights, and rights of racial & ethnic minorities.

International Climate Finance Plan of the US

The US President recently revealed the country's new Finance Plan at the Leader's Summit on Climate. The Summit was hosted by the USA.

Contents
About the Plan

Background

Millennium Change Company

US International Development Finance Corporation

About the Plan

The US has set a new aim to lower its emissions by 50% to 52% as compared to 2005 levels.

The US will quadruple its climate spending by 2024. It aims to treble its climate funding ultimately.

The United States Agency for International Development (USAID) plans to present a new Climate Change Strategy in November 2021 at the COP26.

The United States International Development Finance Corporation intends to adapt its development strategy to incorporate climate in its plan. It will emphasize climate mitigation and adaptability. This is the first time the US is considering the climate in its development plan.

The Millennium Change company will concentrate on climate-wise development and sustainable infrastructure. It seeks to allocate more than 50% of its financing to climate-related initiatives.

The US Treasury will instruct the executive directors at multilateral development institutions such as World Bank to ensure that they establish aggressive climate funding objectives.

The proposal will also concentrate on stopping overseas investments in carbon-intensive fossil fuel-based energy goods.

Background

The United States is the world's second leading emitter behind China. The government would have to provide 800 billion USD as its contribution to the international climate funding.

Millennium Change Company

It is a bilateral foreign US assistance organization that was created in 2004. It gives financial help to nations with excellent economic development via smart policies.

US International Development Finance Corporation

The US International Development Finance Corporation is responsible for providing funding to private development initiatives in low-income and middle-income nations. It was created in 2019.

PESCO: EU allows US participation for the first time

The European Union has accepted the demands of Norway, Canada, and United States to join in the Permanent Structured Cooperation (PESCO) military project. This is the first time; the European bloc has permitted a third state to join the PESCO program. The nations will now join the Military Mobility Project in Europe.

Contents

Neutral States in PESCO

What is PESCO?

It is an element of the European Union's security and defense strategy. It was developed based on the Treaty of the European Union enacted by the Treaty of Lisbon in 2009.

PESCO and NATO

Around four-fifths of the PESCO countries are also NATO members. NATO is North Atlantic Treaty Organisation.

US And PESCO

The United States has voiced concerns about PESCO multiple times. According to commentators, it is a hint that the US fears loss of power in Europe. The US exports 1 billion Euros of armaments to the European Union nations every year.

Military Mobility Project

It aims to assist the unrestricted mobility of military units throughout the European Union via the enhancement of infrastructure and elimination of bureaucratic hurdles. It generally centers on two areas - bureaucratic hurdles (such as passport checks) and the necessity of prior notice. During a NATO emergency, the forces may move freely and fastly. However, during peacetime, early warning is essential.

Background

In November 2020, the European Union permitted non-EU members to join PESCO. Following this, Canada, the US, and Norway sought to join PESCO.

Neutral States in PESCO

Four of the states in the European Union declare themselves neutral. They are Austria, Ireland, Finland, and Sweden.

Anna May Wong – first Asian-American to be featured on US currency

Anna May Wong, a Chinese-American movie actress in Hollywood, is scheduled to become the first Asian American to appear on US currency.

Contents

Key facts

American Women Quarters (AWQ) Program

Key facts

A quarter-dollar coin portraying a close-up portrait of Anna May Wong will start circulation on October 24, 2022.

This will be the sixth coin in the American Women Quarters (AWQ) Program.

It will contain the Latin words "E PLURIBUS UNUM", which means "out of many, one".

It is aimed to celebrate Wong's achievements while overcoming obstacles and barriers throughout her lifetime.

Wong is considered Hollywood's first Chinese-American star, having a decades-long career in motion movies, television, and theatre despite the prevalent bigotry in the United States.

As the first Asian female performer, she endured prejudice and was put aside in favor of non-Asian females.

She was forced to play exoticized stereotypes of East Asians and could not get lead roles in films because of laws prohibiting actors from different races from kissing on screen.

She is famed for dying a thousand deaths due to the villainous roles she played.

Wong received a star on the Hollywood Walk of Fame. She was the first Asian American actress to do so. Lucy Liu became the second Asian American woman to achieve this feat in 2019.

Wong was born in Los Angeles to second-generation Taishanese Chinese-American parents in 1905.

During the silent cinema period, she participated in "The Toll of the Sea" (1922) - one of the earliest color pictures.

American Women Quarters (AWQ) Program

The AWQ program is a four-year initiative that acknowledges the accomplishments of women in the United States from 2022 through 2025. Under this scheme, the US mint will release a series of quarters featuring significant women in United States History. To date, Maya Angelou, Dr. Sally Ride, Wilma Mankiller, and Nina Otero-Warren have been featured in the program.

Foreign Direct Product Rule (FDPR)

The US Government recently imposed FDPR to limit China's access to advanced computer chips and chip-making equipment, which are used for military modernization and the development of weapons of mass destruction.

Contents

Key facts

What is the Foreign Direct Product Rule?

Key facts

The foreign direct product rule (FDPR) was recently applied to China's advanced computing and supercomputer industry to prevent it from obtaining advanced computing chips.

The imposition of the FDPR would prevent companies, including those operating outside American soil, from selling certain products that were produced using American technology to Chinese consumers without the US government's permission.

This law will now apply to semiconductor chips used in supercomputers and some artificial intelligence applications.

It will prevent China from developing nuclear weapons and other military equipment.

The imposition of the new rule would mean that China has to develop its manufacturing technologies and processor technologies to replace the US or Western technologies that are currently being used. It is estimated to take 5 to 10 years for China to catch up with the current technologies.

Earlier, this rule was imposed on Chinese telecom company Huawei to curtail its supply of semiconductors and adversely affect the company's smartphone business.

The rule is currently applied in Russia and Belarus. It was imposed in protest against the invasion of Ukraine.

What is the Foreign Direct Product Rule?

The Foreign Direct Product Rule (FDPR) was introduced in 1959 by the US government to control the trading of US technologies. It prevents and regulates the trade of products (including those made in foreign countries) that were made using US-made technology and software. It mandates country-based licensing requirements and list-based restrictions apart from imposing traditional export controls to weaken the FDPR-targeted countries' ability to obtain critical items produced from US-origin technologies.

Hurricane Ian

Hurricane Ian impacted the US state of Florida.

Contents

 Key facts

About Category 5 Hurricanes

Key facts

Category 4 hurricane Ian struck Florida's southern coast.

As one of the most severe hurricanes in US history, it has blown away houses and structures, leaving some citizens trapped.

It made landfall at Cayo Costa with a maximum sustained wind speed of 150 mph, just 7 mph slower than Category 5 — the highest status on the Saffir-Simpson Hurricane Scale of Hurricane Intensity.

Much of the coastal areas in southwest Florida had power disruptions due to this destructive storm, which generated high-speed winds and floods.

It is projected to significantly affect millions of people in the US states of Florida, Georgia, and South Carolina.

Earlier, this hurricane had caused full power loss in Cuba, after slamming the island as Category 3 storm.

At least two persons have lost their lives due to this hurricane in Cuba.

About Category 5 Hurricanes

Category 5 hurricanes have maximum sustained winds of 157 kilometers per hour or greater. Their occurrence is infrequent in the United States. They have happened just four times in the country's history, all of which slammed the Gulf Coast. One of these hurricanes impacted Mississippi while the others made landfall in Florida. These storms are capable of demolishing a high proportion of framed houses, with catastrophic roof failure and wall collapse. Fallen trees and electrical poles will create isolation in residential areas. The power outages will endure for weeks, if not months. Most of the afflicted locations will become uninhabitable for weeks or months. Currently, climate change is gradually worsening the storms. While climate change may intensify the storms, wind speed, and precipitation, the overall number of storms will not be increased.

Dr. Renee Wegrzyn was chosen as the director of ARPA-H

US President Joe Biden nominated Dr. Renee Wegrzyn as the initial head of the

ARPA-H (Advanced Research Projects Agency for Health) and explained her responsibilities during his address on the 60th anniversary of President John F. Kennedy's moonshot speech at Rice University

Contents

Key facts

60th Anniversary of President Kennedy's Moonshot Address

Key facts

Dr. Renee Wegrzyn, a biologist, and former government scientist was named the first-ever head of the newly founded Advanced Research Projects Agency for Health (ARPA-H) (ARPA-H).

The ARPA-H Director's tenure would last for five years.

The purpose of the ARPA-H is to seek innovative solutions to biomedical problems.

It would support highly risky but rewarding research in the life sciences.

It was established to emulate the US Defense Advanced Research Projects Agency (DARPA), which had played a key role in the rapid development of defense technologies by awarding contracts to risky projects, which can be withdrawn abruptly if the researchers do not meet the desired milestone.

Dr. Renee Wegrzyn served as the program manager at the DARPA for more than 5 years, working on projects that used synthetic biology to counter infectious diseases and boost biosecurity.

Though ARPA-H has a new director, the agency's foundational details are currently lacking.

The US Congress had allocated ARAP-H just 1 billion USD for 2022. The Biden Administration had requested a budget of 6.5 billion USD.

The agency also lacks backing from the legislation specifically authorizing its creation.

60th Anniversary of President Kennedy's Moonshot Address

President Kennedy gave his famous Moonshot Speech on September 12, 1962, at Rice University, Houston. During his address, the President recommitted the US' Moon landing aim that was established in May 1961 to place humans on the lunar surface by the end of the decade and bring them safely back to Earth.

John Lee: Hong Kong's Next Leader

John Lee Ka-Chiu, a former security chief has recently been elected as the next leader of Hong Kong. This move is widely regarded as the Chinese government's move to tighten its grip on the city.

Contents

Who will be replaced by John Lee?

What role did Lee play during the violent crackdowns in 2019?

Why was John Lee economically sanctioned by the United States?

Which party was banned during Lee's watch?

What is his stance on the extradition bill?

Who will be succeeded by John Lee?

Carrie Lam is being replaced by John Lee after the city's chief executive election was held. From 1st July 2022, Lee will begin his five-year term as the city's chief executive.
What role did Lee play during the violent crackdowns in 2019?

In 2019, he was serving as the Secretary for Security when the police started violent crackdowns on the pro-democracy protests. The protests began after a controversial bill was announced that would allow an individual to be extradited to mainland China. Lee permitted Hong Kong's police force to use rubber bullets, tear gas, water cannons, and even at certain times live ammunition on all those who were protesting.

Why was John Lee economically sanctioned by the United States?

In August 2020, the United States placed economic penalties on him for limiting the autonomy of Hong Kong as well as curtailing freedom of speech. This sentence occurred after 2 months after enacting a security bill that criminalized most activists and demonstrations and weakened the judicial sovereignty of Hong Kong. The US accused him of employing force to arrest, pressurize, jail, and detain civilians and of forming a special police unit to enforce the harsh legislation.

Which party was outlawed under Lee's watch?

The Hong Kong National Party was outlawed under Lee's supervision. It was the first party that backed independence for Hong Kong after the British ceded the province to China in the year 1997. This party was prohibited in the year 2018. The party was charged by Lee to have promoted hostility toward mainland China.

What is his view on the extradition bill?

Lee approved the extradition measure owing to which he suffered a lot of backlashes. However, during his election campaign, his attitude about the measure altered, and declared there isn't any need to discuss the extradition law anymore. After the demonstrations and the backlashes, the law was not completely launched.

SIPRI Report on World Military Expenditure

A study by the Stockholm International Peace Research Institute (SIPRI) on World Military Expenditure said that India was the world's third-highest military spender after the US and China. The global defense expenditure in 2021 reached an all-time high and stood at USD 2.1 trillion despite the COVID-19 pandemic.

Contents

Top 5 military spenders

Military spending in India

Military spending across the world

Top 5 military spenders

According to the SIPRI data, the top five military spenders in the world are:

The United States

China

India

The United Kingdom

Russia

The top 5 nations contribute to 62 percent of the world's global military budget.

Military expenditures of India

According to the statistics given by SIPRI, the military budget of India amounted to USD 76.6 billion in 2021, which is a 0.9 percent rise from 2020 and a 33 percent increase from 2012. India is confronting continuing border tensions and disagreements with Pakistan and China that periodically generate military confrontations. Hence, India is constantly modernizing its armed forces and is increasing its self-reliance in the production of armaments.

Military expenditures around the globe

In 2021, the US has accounted for 38 percent of the world's military spending. China accounts for around 14 percent and the UK has moved up two ranks as it spent USD 68.4 billion. According to the report, China's military spending has increased for the 27th year in a row. The growing assertiveness of China in the region of the East and South China seas has become a major military spending driver in countries such as Japan and Australia. Russia also witnessed an increase in its military expenditure for the third year in a row. There was a decline in Russia's military expenditure between 2016 to 2019 due to sanctions that were imposed by the West in response to the annexation of Crimea by Russia. In 2021, high gas and oil revenues helped the country to boost its military spending.

AUKUS: Collaboration on Hypersonic Weapons

Australia, Britain, and the United States will begin working on strengthening military capability and hypersonic missile attacks bearing in mind that their adversaries China and Russia are growing swiftly in cutting-edge defense technologies.

Contents

Overview:

Reason for this partnership

About Hypersonic missiles

Overview:

The three declared their partnership on hypersonic missiles as an outgrowth of the recent defensive alliance of AUKUS.

Under this defensive partnership, Australia will also be armed with nuclear-powered submarines so that they can oppose the expanding military dominance of China.

The trio is partnering to work in the realm of hypersonic and counter-hypersonic missiles as well as expanding the capabilities of electronic warfare.

Reason for this partnership

Russia is now the most advanced in the area of hypersonic missiles with China also expanding its capabilities. To counter this, the AUKUS has come together to improve its skills in this sector.

About Hypersonic missiles

A hypersonic missile is a sort of weapon system that flies at the speed of Mach 5 and may be maneuvered. The maneuvering capabilities of this missile are what differentiates it from a ballistic missile. A ballistic missile follows a defined course whereas hypersonic missiles may be maneuvered to achieve an intended target. This maneuverability capability of this missile makes it difficult to intercept and they can carry nuclear as well as conventional warheads.

US-EU Agreement on Data Transfer Pact

The United States and the European Union have announced that they have an "in principle" agreement in place to create a new framework for cross-border data transfers.

Contents

Overview:

Invalidation of Privacy Shield

About the new accord

Respite to the tech companies

Overview:

This announcement has come as a much-needed relief for various tech giants like Google and Meta.
For more than a year, officials have been planning out a deal to replace the invalidated Privacy Shield, an arrangement that allows firms to share European data with the U.S.

Invalidation of Privacy Shield

In July 2020, the Privacy Shield was invalidated. This struck a blow to the tech companies that were relying on this mechanism for the US-EU data flow. The top court of the EU sided with privacy activist Max Schrems who had argued that the existing framework did not protect the people living in Europe from surveillance by the United States.

About the new accord

This newly established framework underlines the dedication towards data protection, privacy, and its associated policies. A seamless flow of data between the EU and the US would aid in facilitating business interactions equal to USD 7.1 trillion. This agreement will also aid in allowing the trustworthiness and predictability of data transfers across the Atlantic, thereby guaranteeing the privacy of all persons.

Respite to the tech businesses

This recently announced agreement would give some reprieve for the digital businesses that were experiencing legal ambiguity in transferring data across borders after the decision to do away with Privacy Shield was made. Meta has claimed that it would even have to shut down Instagram and Facebook in Europe over the matter of Privacy Shield.

Australia, Britain, and the United States will begin working on strengthening military capability and hypersonic missile attacks bearing in mind that their adversaries China and Russia are growing swiftly in cutting-edge defense technologies.

Overview:

Reason for this partnership

About Hypersonic missiles

Overview:

The three declared their partnership on hypersonic missiles as an outgrowth of the recent defensive alliance of AUKUS.

Under this defensive partnership, Australia will also be outfitted with nuclear-powered submarines so that they can oppose the expanding military dominance of China.

The trio is partnering to work in the realm of hypersonic and counter-hypersonic missiles as well as expanding the capabilities of electronic warfare.

Reason for this partnership

Russia is now the most advanced in the area of hypersonic missiles with China also expanding its capabilities. To counter this, the AUKUS has come together to improve its skills in this sector.

About Hypersonic missiles

A hypersonic missile is a sort of weapon system that flies at the speed of Mach 5 and may be maneuvered. The maneuvering capabilities of this missile are what differentiates it from a ballistic missile. A ballistic missile follows a defined course whereas hypersonic missiles may be maneuvered to achieve an intended target. The maneuvering capabilities of this missile make it tough to intercept and they may carry nuclear as well as conventional payloads.

The instructions for the implementation of the Positive Pay System were released by the RBI for the banks of the nation. From 1st January 2021, this method has been deployed to secure banks from any cheque fraud.

Overview:

How does this system work?

Amount Limit

Overview:

The National Payments Corporation of India has established the Positive Pay System.

Through this technique, the details of high-value cheques are reconfirmed.

Through this system, precautions are made to identify any cheque transaction-related fraudulent activity.

How does this system work?

While submitting a high-value check, the person additionally sends various facts about the cheque such as date, account number, amount, cheque number, beneficiary name, transaction code, and

MICR CODE. This information may be supplied by mobile app, SMS, ATM, online banking, and even by visiting the branch. The information is then cross-checked when the cheque is being issued and any inconsistency detected is highlighted. In case of any discovered differences, the bank informs the drawer and withholds any payment until a further order is received.

Amount Limit

The RBI has asked the banks in the nation to provide this service for all account holders that are issuing checks of sums of Rs 50,000 and above. The availing of this feature is at the account holder's choice but the banks may make it obligatory in the event of cheques that have values of Rs 5,00,000 and more.

Nepal: Approval of US Aid Grant

The parliament of Nepal has accepted a disputed USD 500million US gift, despite resistance and mass demonstrations from the Communist parties. In 2017, the US government's Millennium Challenge Corporation (MCC) deal was signed by Nepal for infrastructure projects but its ratification had been on hold as there were differences between political parties, including the coalition that was governing.

Overview:

About Millennium Challenge Corporation

Overview:

Prime Minister Sher Bahadur Deuba's coalition partners expressed strong opposition, stating that this treaty undermined Nepal's sovereignty.

As part of a compromise, the vote contained a proclamation indicating that Nepal would not join any strategic, security, or military, alliance, including the United States Indo-Pacific Strategy.

There were also reports blaming China for the dissemination of disinformation surrounding this treaty.

About Millennium Challenge Corporation

The Millennium Challenge Corporation (MCC) is a United States bilateral foreign assistance organization formed in 2004 by the US Congress. It is a distinct agency from the USAID and State Department. It grants funding to nations that have been assessed to have the potential for economic development and solid economic policies. The nation-qualifying technique is objective, involving scores in 20 distinct categories given by third parties. A nation that is qualified for a grant must apply with a particular project in mind. This organization is based in Washington D.C.

SWIFT Ban on Russia

The United States and the European Union (EU) have agreed to shut off several Russian banks from SWIFT, the key international payment system. Russia's central bank assets will also be blocked, which would restrict Moscow's ability to access its overseas reserves.

Overview:

Before Russia, has any nation been shut off from SWIFT?

How many Russian banks have been shut off from SWIFT?

How will this action affect Russia?

About SWIFT

Overview:

This move's objective is to further isolate Russia from the international financial system bearing in mind the Russian invasion of Ukraine.

These penalties are the harshest against Moscow since its soldiers invaded Ukraine. This is likely to have a huge effect on Russia which depends considerably on the SWIFT infrastructure for its natural resource trading, such as gas and oil exports.

In the financial sector, shutting a nation off from SWIFT is similar to blocking a country's Internet access.

Before Russia, has any nation been shut off from SWIFT?

Before Russia, Iran was the only nation that was shut off from SWIFT. Being shut off from SWIFT resulted in losing a third of Iran's international trade earnings.

How many Russian banks have been shut off from SWIFT?

As of yet, the move against Russia has only been partly executed, with just a few Russian banks getting the penalties. The prospect of widening the punishment to a pan-country ban is being held back by of now the US and its allies as a further escalatory measure.

How will this action affect Russia?
Excluding Russian banks from the SWIFT network would have a hugely detrimental effect on the country's economy. Only a few banks have been targeted to leave the option of future escalation open while also ensuring that the sanctions have the biggest possible effect on Moscow while avoiding a large impact on European firms who engage with Russian banks for their gas import

payments. Also, the limits on Russia's central bank will prohibit Moscow from utilizing its foreign currency reserves to lessen the effect of sanctions.

About SWIFT

The society for Worldwide Interbank Financial Telecommunication (SWIFT) system is a secure platform that is used by numerous financial institutions to transmit information connected to worldwide monetary transactions including money transfers.

SWIFT does not directly transfer money around. Instead, it functions as a middleman by offering secure financial communications services for more than 11,000 institutions situated in over 200 countries. SWIFT is situated in Belgium and central banks from 11 nations monitor it.

The nations are France, Canada, Italy, Germany, the Netherlands, Japan, Switzerland, Sweden, the United States, the United Kingdom, and Belgium.

US-EU Agreement on Data Transfer Pact

The United States and the European Union have claimed that they have an "in principle" agreement in place to build a new framework for cross-border data transfers.

Overview:

Invalidation of Privacy Shield

About the new accord

Respite to the tech businesses

Overview:

This revelation has come as a much-needed relief for different tech companies like Google and Meta.

For more than a year, authorities have been drawing out an agreement to replace the invalidated Privacy Shield, a mechanism that lets corporations exchange European data with the U.S.

Invalidation of Privacy Shield

In July 2020, the Privacy Shield was invalidated. This delivered a blow to the IT businesses that were depending on this system for the US-EU data flow. The highest court of the EU agreed with privacy campaigner Max Schrems who had contended that the present framework did not protect the individuals residing in

Europe from monitoring by the United States.

About the new accord

This newly established framework underlines the dedication towards data protection, privacy, and its associated policies. A seamless flow of data between the EU and the US would aid in facilitating business interactions equal to USD 7.1 trillion. This agreement will also aid in allowing the trustworthiness and predictability of data transfers across the Atlantic, thereby guaranteeing the privacy of all persons.

Respite to the tech businesses

This recently announced agreement would give some reprieve for the digital businesses that were experiencing legal ambiguity in transferring data across borders after the decision to do away with Privacy Shield was made. Meta has claimed that it would even have to shut down Instagram and Facebook in Europe over the matter of Privacy Shield.

Nord Stream 2

The Nord Stream 2 is a 1,200-km pipeline that stretches, via the Baltic Sea, from Ust-Luga in Russia to Greifswald in Germany. This pipeline will be transporting 55 billion cubic meters of gas yearly. In the year 2015, the decision to develop this pipeline was decided.

Overview:

Controversies over Nord Stream 2

Significance of Nord Stream 2

Overview:

The Nord Stream 1 pipeline has already been constructed and coupled with the Nord Stream 2, Germany will be supplied with 110 billion cubic meters of gas a year.

The decision to develop Nord Stream 2 was taken up by Gazprom, the Russian energy behemoth, and five other corporations in Europe.

The Nord Stream 2 is priced at roughly USD 11 billion.

The Nord Stream 2 pipeline will operate parallelly with Nord Stream 1.

The pipeline is about 98 percent built and passes through European Union nations Germany and Denmark.

Controversies over Nord Stream 2

The United States has been critical of the Nord Stream 2 pipeline. It thinks that this project would enhance Europe's dependency on Russia for natural gas, therefore emboldening Russian President Vladimir Putin. Currently, the EU countries depend on Russia for 40% of their demand for natural gas.

This initiative is also opposed in Eastern Europe, notably, Ukraine whose relationship with Russia has worsened with a conflict taking place. A pipeline already exists that links Europe and Russia through Ukraine. Hence, Ukraine fears that once Nord 2 is built it will fully be bypassed and the transit charge payment of USD 3 billion would be refused to them.

The Donald Trump administration adopted a bill imposing penalties against any EU corporation working on the Nord Stream 2 project. The Biden administration, while opposed to the pipeline, had considered waiving the sanctions to enhance its diplomatic connections with Germany, but with the looming invasion of Ukraine by Russia, the sanctions will be continuing.

Significance of Nord Stream 2
Germany relies on other nations for the import of Gas and Oil. This pipeline will assist stabilize the situation as Germany is increasingly oriented towards a steady industrial sector and wants to progressively transition towards renewable sources of energy.

Through this pipeline, Europe will be obtaining a steady supply of gas, while, Russia would receive direct access to the European market.

Nord Stream 2's planned route uses the Exclusive Economic Zone (EEZ) and territorial seas of Sweden, Finland, and Denmark. This will aid the national governments of these nations via investments and employment development. This pipeline will give stability to the energy trade since there will be a rise in Russia's dependency on Europe and vice-versa. The Nord Stream 2 pipeline is also projected to lower gas prices.

US Bill on Rare Earth supplies

The United States Government has lately introduced a law to eliminate China's "chokehold" on rare–earth metal supply.
Why the bill?

Aim of the bill

Features of the bill

Rare Earth Metals

Current Scenario

Why the bill?

Rare earth metals are employed practically in every contemporary technology going from electric batteries to combat planes. China has a significant chokehold on all these metals. In 2019, 80% of the US rare−earth metals came from China.

Aim of the bill

The bill aims to reduce the Chinese dependence on rare−earth metals. This is necessary to shield the US from the danger of rare−earth metal supply interruption. It will encourage the locals to expand domestic production of rare−earth metals. Ultimately it will diminish the US dependency on China.

Features of the bill

The law encourages to development of a strategic reserve for rare earth elements. The reserve should be maintained by the Department of Defence and Interiors. The reserve shall fulfill the demands of the IT industry, the US army, and other key infrastructure needs.

The capacity of the stockpile should fulfill American rare–earth metal demands for one year.

It has requested the Commerce Department to investigate unfair trade practices in China.

The bill aims to provide higher transparency on the origin of the components.

It also restricts the use of Chinese rare–earth metals in sophisticated defense equipment.

Rare Earth Metals

Rare earth metals are the 17 metals in the periodic table. They are the 15 lanthanides and scandium and yttrium. They are mainly used in high-tech devices such as mobile phones, flat-screen monitors and televisions, and electric and hybrid vehicles. They are also essential in defense applications such as radar, lasers, sonar systems, and electronic displays.

Current Scenario

In 1993, the US accounted for 38% of world rare earth production and China contributed 33%. Now China contributes to 97% of rare earth metal production in the world.

Printed in Great Britain
by Amazon

24416013R00071